Dog

pawsonality test

Dog
pawsonality
test

Alison Davies

Illustrated by Alissa Levy

WHITE LION
PUBLISHING

Contents

Introduction

Dogs lift the spirits, just by being DOG. Their enthusiastic tail wag, irresistible puppy dog eyes, loyal nature and need to please have secured their place as man's best friend. From the first wolves which hunted alongside early man during the Ice Age, they may have initially competed for food but it soon became clear that working together had its benefits. Over time they were domesticated by hunter-gatherers who recognized the power and strength of their canine cohorts and, through breeding, evolved them into dogs.

Today our dogs are fully fledged family members, taking centre stage in our lives and filling them with joy. But what really makes your pooch tick? It might seem like they wear their hearts on their sleeves, and that their deepest passions are belly rubs, afternoon naps and treats. Yet dig a little a deeper and you'll find that there are lots of things we *think* we know and perhaps even more that we don't.

Do our pups *really* bark at nothing or are they dictating their orders doggy style? Are they chasing their own tails or trying to hypnotize us? And for what covert operation did they learn that marine-style side-to-side belly crawl? Mystified? They might be too. With a brain the size of a tangerine, there's plenty of space for confusion, chaos and lots of loving face licks. From fur baby to fearless and back in 30 seconds, your dog is an enigma, and while you may never know the full story, there is rhyme to their reason. With this doggy decoder, you can dig beneath the surface to get an understanding of who your pup really is. After all, your pooch lives to make you happy, so it's only fair you return the favour. The more you know about their personality type, the more you'll be able to help them live their best puppin' life by being their best human. You'll also understand which training tips and tricks are sure to get your pooch a-woofin' and a-waggin' – and who doesn't want that?

It can take a lifetime to suss out your Spaniel or work out what makes your Terrier tick, so it helps to have a starting point, and that's exactly what you'll find within these pages – a base from which to explore your pup's pawsonality and crack the canine code.

How To Use This Book

Each of the nine quizzes in this book examines a different area of your canine's pawsonality. Pick a quiz topic and simply choose which answer from A to D most resonates with your pooch. Add up the letters at the end to discover which of the four profiles is your pup's best match.

Intrigued to know what part breed plays when it comes to your pup's particular quirks? On pages 122–125 you can learn a bit more about popular breeds and their typical personality matches. Is your pooch more nature than nurture, or does your miniature Poodle have all the steel and grit of a more formidable breed like a Rottweiler?

While this book is based on research, it is not a scientific book, but rather a fun guide to help you understand your dog and better cultivate the bond with your pet. Dogs are full of surprises, so don't worry if you don't end up with definitive answers. As you work through the different tests, you will discover just how multi-faceted your pooch really is.

The Six Canine Characteristics

Each profile also suggests which of the six major personality traits (see right) – first listed by the American Kennel Club in 1979 and adapted slightly to suit today's canines – best fit your dog. Add these up as you go through all nine tests, keeping score on page 118, and find out which ones feature the most in your pup's overall personality. This will give you a fully rounded picture of your pooch.

The Six Canine Characteristics

2

WELL-BALANCED

A friendly and sociable pooch, she loves to be at the heart of the family.

3

EXTROVERT

This confident mutt actively seeks out new experiences and likes to take the lead.

1

DOMINANT

This is a forceful pup who is not afraid to assert himself in most situations.

4

INTROVERT

This nervous pooch needs reassurance and will form a close bond with her owner.

5

ADAPTABLE

Gentle and affectionate, this pup may lack confidence but he's easy to handle and is co-operative.

6

INDEPENDENT

With little interest in human companionship, this mutt thrives when given a sense of purpose.

Top Dog

How Are Your Dog's Confidence Levels?

Dogs have primal instincts which power them through the ranks in the pack. These impulses, developed at birth, mean that some dogs are natural leaders, while others are followers. Dominant pups get the first look in when vying for their mother's attention and, over time, each pup finds its place in the pack as their instincts develop.

Where your dog sits in the greater hierarchy is partly down to early conditioning, as well as the way in which they fit into your family dynamic. Personality also plays a big part, and overly anxious or introverted pups will be less confident. Breed, too, has a role to play, but while you might assume bigger dogs are dominant and boss material, the truth is some smaller breeds also have CEO potential.

Not every pooch wants to be Top Dog; some prefer to follow, and some to mediate, letting the natural born leaders direct from the front. Identifying where your pooch sits on the Alpha to Omega scale can reveal amazing insights into their psyche. Are they planning world domination or just trying to monopolize the sofa you're occupying?

Q1. **There's a family dynamic in every household, and your dog will fit in there somewhere. So how does your pooch think of you?**

    A   As his partner in crime.

    B   As his best bud.

    C   As his ma or pa.

    D   As a member of 'his' pack.

Q2. **When it comes to film night, who gets the top spot on the sofa?**

    A   She's happy to let you have it, as long as she can sidle up.

    B   She doesn't care, she'll find the perfect snoozing spot somewhere close.

    C   You do, but with her curled on your lap.

    D   She does, and when you try to move her, she plays dead.

Q3. How does your pooch make new puppy pals?

A Gradually, with a lot of bottom sniffing involved.

B Easily, there's lots of rubbing up close and excited yapping.

C He's super shy, and it takes a long time before he trusts another dog.

D They're not pals, they're subordinates!

Q4. There's a face-off between your dog and another. What's the likely outcome?

A It's all about the bark, and she's not afraid to use it.

B She'll avoid confrontation but will stand her ground if she has to.

C She'll hide behind you, a lamppost, a blade of grass – you get the picture …

D Nothing scares this mutt: SHE IS THE QUEEN.

Q5. Does your dog share the love, or is he a one-person pooch?

A He's happy to meet new people, but you'll always be his favourite human.

B He's friendly with everyone.

C Other people? What are they? He's got you and that's all that counts.

D He'll put up with people, as long as they know their place.

Q6. **It's your pooch's favourite roast chicken dinner. How does she behave?**

A She takes flight with a chicken wing.

B She'll kill you with kindness and head rubs until she gets a piece.

C She'll lick her lips and dribble until you feel so bad you give in.

D She's at the head of the dinner table, naturally!

Q7. **If your mutt was part of a larger doggy crew, what would his position be in the pack?**

A He'd be up there leading the way to new adventures.

B He'd be everyone's pooch pal and part of the team.

C He'd feel safer in the background taking orders.

D He's Top Dog, puller of strings and king of everything.

Q8. **Which television mutt does your dog most resemble in their attitude?**

A Sassy, like Brian Griffin.

B Cheerful, like Santa's Little Helper.

C Scared, like Scooby Doo.

D In charge, like Snoopy.

Q9. In a room full of children, what would your pooch do?

A   Chase his tail and run riot with the kids.

B   Make sure all the little ones get a chance for a stroke and a cuddle.

C   Whimper and hide in a corner.

D   Pace the perimeter to avoid sticky prodding fingers.

The Results

The Renegade

WELL-BALANCED & EXTROVERT

Cheeky is this canine's middle name. To her life's one big game, and she likes to play her part. She's friendly and fun, the life and soul of the party without a doubt, but that doesn't mean she won't holler if something's not right. She's no walkover when it comes to her mates, but what happens between mutts and butts stays right where it is. Once she's sussed out who's who and what's what, she'll be back to her usual happy self. As far as humans are concerned, she only has eyes for you. Being up there in the family crew is what makes this dog's tail wag, but just in case you get too comfortable she'll throw in a canine curveball every now and then. Expect things to go missing and turn up chewed. It's all part of her masterplan to keep you entertained – and under the paw.

The Team Player

WELL-BALANCED & ADAPTABLE

Relaxed, chillaxed and definitely not taxed, this boy likes an easy life and why not? Let the Alpha dogs puff their chests and give it their best. When it comes to ruffling feathers or fur, he'd sooner lie on the floor and chew his squeaky toy. He takes it all in his puppy dog stride. Most likely a gentle, easy-going breed like a Bichon Frise or a King Charles Spaniel, he's everyone's best bud, and the one you can count on when you need a pick-me-up. If this pooch could talk, he'd be all about the middle ground. The Team Player is clever too; not only can he read your moods and needs, he knows a tummy roll *always* succeeds when it comes to extra treats. His motto is 'Kill 'em with kindness', and if all else fails, he'll concede defeat, as long as it's curled up at your feet.

Top Dog

The Puppy

INTROVERT & ADAPTABLE

This anxious little soul just loves to be nurtured. It's not her fault; she's likely to be the runt of the litter and finds it hard to make her voice heard. Sweet and snuggly are her superpowers. This mutt melts the hardest of hearts, but don't expect her to stand her ground. She'll flee at the sight of a fight or find a way to hide – whether that's under the sofa or up your jumper, she doesn't care as long as you're there. She needs lots of reassurance and looks to you for leadership. You're the Alpha to her Omega, and the burger to her bun. With a wet nose and woeful eyes, she knows how to pull at the heartstrings, but that's fine with you. Nerves aside, this pooch is a true gem. All she needs is a little extra love to help her shine.

The Captain

DOMINANT & EXTROVERT

This boy's the Boss with a capital B. He leads from the front and takes no prisoners. Strong, sturdy and steadfast, if he wants something, he gets it – end of discussion. The Captain might be a handful, but with some careful training to curb his ego, he'll stay close to heel. At home he likes to be Top Dog, securing the best spot in front of the TV and turfing you from your bed. That said, he'll usually acquiesce, especially if there's a treat involved or some cuddle time. This boy's a big softy at heart – just don't tell the rest of the pack! Most likely an intelligent breed, like a Rottweiler or a German Shepherd, Captains come in all shapes and sizes. What counts is what's on the inside, and the teeniest of dogs can harbour a steely resolve beneath the fur and fluff. If you've got a Captain in your life, give him free rein at play and let him know who's boss within the home by defining boundaries and standing your ground when he tries to take over.

Top Dog

21

Dozing Doggy Style

What Are Your Dog's Sleeping Patterns?

Dogs and dozing are good bedfellows, and who wouldn't want to snuggle up and catch a few zzzz? Our canines have turned the afternoon nap into an art form, with the average dog craving around fourteen hours of sleep a day. Some need more, with small toy breeds like Pugs and much larger dogs like Mastiffs napping for up to eighteen hours a day.

You might think your dog is being lazy, but it's actually an important part of their day, and good for health and wellbeing. Expect those with short noses, such as Pugs or Bulldogs, to have you turning up the volume on the TV to compete with the snoring. This tends to get worse as your pet gets older, especially if you allow your pup to pile on the pounds.

Some dogs are light sleepers; they might look as if they're lost in the land of nod, but they're quick to rouse. Whether it's the scent of a meaty burger that gets their nose twitching or the jingle of a lead, they're back in the blink of an eye, while others just love a slumber party. Whatever the deal with your dog's sleep routine, you can learn more about what makes them tick from how, when and where they like to nap.

Q1. An off-the-cuff snooze can result in some wacky sleeping spots. Where's the weirdest place you've found your pooch taking a nap?

A Wedged under the fridge door, in case it accidentally opens and a treat falls out!

B In between the sofa cushions, bottom in the air.

C Head on your lap, shoulder, foot ... any part of you that can take the drool.

D Flat out, face down, in the dirty laundry.

Q2. When does your pup like to catch some zzzz?

A She loves a good snooze in the afternoon sun.

B She's an opportunist napper; she'll grab five minutes here and there.

C She likes to doze in the evening during your fix of Netflix.

D She'd sleep all day if she could!

Q3. You'll never know exactly what your dog dreams of, but as the one who knows him best, you can take a guess! When your dog is in dreamland, he likes to ...

A Chomp on a juicy steak.

B Run and run and run.

C Cuddle up with his human.

D Sleep some more!

Dozing Doggy Style

Q4. What's your dog's favourite dozing position?

   A   Flat on her back, legs akimbo.

   B   She's a contortionist, so in a knot of limbs.

   C   Curled up foetal style, in a snuggly ball.

   D   Sprawled on her tummy.

Q5. Some dogs like to lie beneath the stars, while others steal the duvet. Where does your pooch prefer to sleep?

   A   Near the sweet scent of a warm oven with a roast chicken inside!

   B   Al fresco, on a patch of grass.

   C   On or in your bed.

   D   In front of a roaring fire.

Q6. Is your pup an early riser or a night owl who finds it hard to settle?

   A   She's up as soon as her tummy starts rumbling!

   B   This twitchy tyke finds it hard to calm down, so late nights all round.

   C   She likes a lie in … and an early night.

   D   This laidback lovely is happy to rise and rest when you do.

Q7. You can tell a lot about your pooch's sleep style from their general demeanour. Is your dog a chilled-out canine or a hyper hound?

A This boy's a simple pup – as long as he's fed and watered, he sleeps like a baby.

B Happy, snappy and always super yappy, this energetic pup can struggle to wind down…

C Keep him loved up and he'll stay calm, collected and ready for bed.

D Nothing ruffles this laidback lad; he's the king of chill and could sleep anywhere.

Q8. What funny things does your pooch do while she's in the land of nod?

A She's a fully-fledged farting machine.

B This mutt gets her freak on, twisting, shaking and getting jiggy with it.

C She's the queen of drool, and there's usually a pool of it nearby.

D This pooch likes to shake the foundations with her snoring.

Dozing Doggy Style

27

Q9. **Does your pooch prefer a solo snooze or is he a mutt that likes to lounge around with others?**

A This boy is all about comfort and warmth, and more canine bodies means more of both!

B Snuggling up does nothing for this pup; he likes to go it alone.

C He'll happily doze in your arms, but he's averse to furry charms.

D This pup finds the peace in any situation: with dogs, cats, children or toys!

The Results

The Tyke

EXTROVERT & ADAPTABLE

This girl knows what she needs, and how to get it. Sleep, along with a full belly, is top of her list of essentials. For her, the two go paw in paw. No grumbling tums here: first stop the fridge, and then the dinner table. If that's not forthcoming, she'll win you over with her puppy dog stare. Once the appetite is satiated, she'll happily slip into a cosy slumber filled with dreams of BBQ nibbles and cheesy delights. Comfort is key to this lovable mutt; it makes her feel safe, secure and needed, so while her character stands out from the crowd, along with her belly, the most important thing is her relationship with you and the rest of her pack. This pooch likes to make you feel loved with lots of dribbly kisses; after all, you are her favourite pillow, and you make a pretty good mattress too.

Dozing Doggy Style

B

The Workaholic

WELL-BALANCED & EXTROVERT

Sleep? What's that? This dog hasn't got time to lose, never mind snooze. He's on a mission. With people to see and things to do, leaves to chase and other pups to race, life is a never-ending adventure. Bristling with energy, this pooch keeps you on your toes and there's no chance of him slowing down. The reason for his behaviour is likely a mix of his breed, young age and inquisitive nature. He doesn't want to miss a thing! When he does stop, it's not by choice, it's the need to refuel that makes him take five. He'll grab a nap and be out for the count, but the minute he's topped up, he's back, poised on all paws and looking for trouble. Keep your mutt entertained with games that give him something to chase and lots of walks. Most likely a hyper Hound, or a twitchy Terrier, whatever flavour he rocks, this boy only stops when he's about to drop.

C

The Bedfellow

WELL-BALANCED & INTROVERT

This lady's heart is where you're at. You are her security blanket and the one thing she needs for a restful sleep. She might not be the strongest or fastest dog on the block, but what she lacks in action she more than makes up for in snuggles. The reason she loves her bed so much is not just because she's lazy, it's reassurance that she seeks. She's a puppy at heart and still finding her feet, but when she's curled up with you, all's right with the world. Throw in a couch, some squidgy cushions and a few foodie treats, and she'll be putty in your hands. Likely to be one of the companion breeds, such as a Golden Retriever, this sofa surfer is easy to please, but you can encourage her to be a bit more active with fun games and lots of fuss. Want to make her feel like Top Dog? That's easy: indulge her loving nature and snuggle up with your pup!

The Lounger

WELL-BALANCED & ADAPTABLE

Nothing fazes this boy. He's the king of zen, from the tips of his ears to each gentle paw as it graces the floor. 'Quick' is not a word in his woof-cabulary, neither is 'rush' nor 'stress'. When sleep beckons, he's there in a shot, but it's the only thing he does at speed. He's probably a larger dog breed and his caring nature makes him the ideal companion, especially if you're lazing in the sun. While he likes a good snooze, bedtime is not the be all and end all. He prefers to doze throughout the day, thanks to his chilled-out persona, and if he's a larger lad, he'll need more than the average pooch. So don't despair, just be there for when he comes round for a cuddle. He'll fall where he stands, and sleep where he lands, and that's just the way he rolls …

Where There's a Woof There's a Way

How Does Your Dog Communicate?

You don't have to be Dr Doolittle to have a conversation with your pup. Communication comes in many forms and dogs are experts at the non-verbal kind. They speak to us every day in their own unique way; from the twitch of an ear to the way they hold their derriere, it's all there for us to see and read. The more time you spend with your pooch in different situations, the more you'll start to learn their lingo and understand when they're feeling anxious, excitable or uncomfortable.

Nuances of sound can also reveal when your dog's a happy mutt. Every bark is different, a distinct doggy calling card. Some extrovert breeds really like to chat. Huskies are a prime example: bred to work together in a pack, they'll use their voice to motivate each other, so don't be surprised if they use the same tactics on you. Yorkshire Terriers also make up for what they lack in size with mighty lungs. These belters prove that tiny doesn't always mean whiny.

Whether it's down to their breed, their nature or nurture, how your pooch talks to you can reveal much about their pawsonality and the image they like to present to the world.

Q1. How does your pooch say, 'Good Morning'?

A   Some gentle yapping and lots of doggy breath in the face.

B   He's on the bed and under the duvet before the alarm!

C   He heads straight in for a face lick.

D   He almost bowls you over, following it up with lots of excited yelping.

Q2. How does your dog say hello to other pooches?

A   She heads straight for the bottom for a quick sniff.

B   She shies away from contact and takes her time sussing them out.

C   A whiff of the nose and face is her first approach.

D   Lots of barking and jumping up and down to say, 'I'm here!'

Q3. Dogs can be noisy for lots of reasons. Some like to howl at the moon or yap at the television, while others prefer a quiet life. What gets your mutt barking?

A Other dogs. He likes to be part of the canine choir.

B Sirens, fireworks, a loud commercial ... he hates it all.

C He's not much of a howler. It's all about the tilt of the head and his posture.

D The full moon. This boy's senses prickle at the slightest thing!

Q4. Your pooch likes to stick to routine, and always lets you know when it's treat o'clock with ...

A A series of soulful barks and lots of dribbling.

B A quick woof to get your attention, before eyeing her food bowl.

C A delicate paw on the knee to say 'pleeeeease!'

D Standing by the treat cupboard and yapping loudly until you get the message.

Q5. When you're happy, your canine companion is likely to feel it too. What does he do to share his joy?

A Rolls around yelping and playing the fool.

B Rubs against you with glee.

C Showers you in a pool of drool.

D Dances like a doggy diva.

Q6. **If your pooch is feeling poorly, she will ...**

A Curl up and whimper.

B Retreat to a quiet hidey-hole away from everything.

C Try to let you know with a gentle nudge and lots of lip licking.

D Say 'I feel woof, woof, woof' until you take notice.

Q7. **What does your dog do when you talk to him?**

A Leaps on your lap for a snuggle.

B Cocks his head on one side and listens intently.

C Presses a wet nose against you, as a show of understanding.

D Talks back, with a stream of non-stop yelps.

Q8. **Your dog's bark is as individual as herself. It's her calling card, so what type of barker is she?**

A She's the Mariah Carey of canines, a real high-pitched warbler.

B Bright and cheery, when she does it, she does it with style.

C Squeaky, whiny and tiny, a bit like her.

D Throaty and gruff, she's the raucous rock chick of the doggy kingdom.

Where There's a Woof There's a Way

39

Q9. **Is your pooch up for a chinwag with any waif or stray, or does he hold his tongue when meeting strangers?**

A This crafty canine uses sound and high-vaulting acrobatics to astound his audience.

B This pup knows head rubs and snuffles win friends and hearts.

C This quiet lad likes to keep shtum if you're not his chum.

D No softly, softly for this chatterer, he'll natter away loudly with anyone who'll listen.

The Results

The Clown

EXTROVERT & ADAPTABLE

This class clown loves goofing around and has a range of quirky sounds at her disposal. She's fairly easy to read because she couples noise with poise and facial expression. Her doggy demeanour is usually calm and friendly, so when something's afoot you'll know. With a flexible face and a sense of grace, you'll swear she's smiling at you, just by the way her mouth curves up. This pleasant pup doesn't get easily rattled, and while you may hear her bark and yelp, she saves it for those times when she really needs to get her message across. The Clown is fun to be around. She'll entertain you and make you smile when life's getting you down, and makes it easy for you to decipher her canine code. Together you're the A team when it comes to communication. She 'gets' you, and you 'get' her – you're the perfect pair!

B

The Guru

WELL-BALANCED & ADAPTABLE

This charming boy might seem like an old soul to you. He doesn't say much, but what he does say, he makes it count. His body language is second to none, and a tool he uses to read situations and let you know how he feels. When he turns his attention on you, you'll know. Those puppy peepers have a power that draws you in, and with a single expression you'll feel what's in his heart. Gentle, wise and always by your side, he knows what you are thinking before you do, and while you can take some time to catch on, he's already ahead of the game. The more time you spend with him, the more in tune you'll be. Just take your time and follow his lead. He'll let you know what he needs in a subtle way. The Guru speaks volumes without opening his mouth. His cautious, careful approach means that when he makes friends, he makes them for life – you included.

The Wallflower

INTROVERT & ADAPTABLE

Where There's a Woof There's a Way

This girl doesn't give much away, unless you know where to look. She's a nervous pup with a heart of gold, but she needs a little encouragement to bare her soul. She's rarely vocal, and you might wonder if she has a voice at all, but this lady prefers to stay shtum. No singing for her supper here, just lots of love and snuggles until you get the gist of what's at the top of her list. Naturally shy, she prefers to demonstrate how she feels with actions. She'll lick and drool to show she's hungry for food and love, and even give the paw to get your attention and open the fridge door. It can be hard to read her at times; you have to watch and learn how she reacts in different situations. Get to know the way she moves and look for clues in her stance, and she'll find a way to show her thanks.

The Chatterbox

WELL-BALANCED & EXTROVERT

This dude knows it's rude not to join in the chat. There's nothing he loves more than expressing himself, in as many ways as he can. Highly vocal, he's a non-stop music machine, and he thrives in a busy atmosphere. Confident and excitable, he just loves life and wants to share the joy. If he's your boy, you'll be in no doubt of how he's feeling at any given moment during the day. He's fairly easy to read, and he has a knack for getting your attention. While his constant chatter might be irritating at times, you can calm him down by playing games and engaging his active brain. Most likely a Husky, Terrier or even a tiny Chihuahua, he likes to be a key part of the family. Lots of fuss will have him eating out of your hand, and firm but soothing words should help to turn down the volume.

Where There's a Woof There's a Way

45

It's a Dog's Life

How Does Your Dog Feel About Their Daily Routine?

Just like humans, every pooch is a one-off, with quirks and character traits that set them apart from the rest of the pack. While personality is influenced by breed, there's so much more that goes into the puppy pot to create your canine. Daily habits play a big part in shaping the way your dog acts and reacts, forming those cute quirks that seem to come from out of the blue.

Your dog's day-to-day doings and the way they do them can help you learn more about the way they roll. Some pups love routine, while others crave the freedom to do their doggy thing. From tennis balls to curve balls that are sure to set the tail wagging, life is never straightforward and a dog's attitude and approach to big and little changes in routine can help you unlock the canine conundrum. Once you understand your mutt's persona, you'll be able to help them live their best life. You can help introverted pups prepare for big and stressful events by practising separation techniques, and for those that get super excited, you can learn how to soothe their spirits to put the bow in their wow!

Q1. If he could, what would your pup spend most of his day doing?

A Playing, walking and spending time with his favourite human.

B Dozing in the sunshine.

C Snuggling up in a small and cosy place.

D Chasing anything that moves.

Q2. What's the strangest thing your dog has eaten?

A Grass, it's just there begging to be nibbled.

B Cake, she likes to partake in your coffee mornings.

C Her own poop, on occasion, just to make a statement.

D Your sweaty socks are her food heaven.

Q3. When an unexpected visitor turns up at your door, what kind of greeting will they get from your mutt?

A He'll be friendly; he loves to meet new people.

B He's not bothered either way, as long as he can do his own thing.

C He goes from crazy yappy to fearful Fido in 0–2 seconds.

D If they're interesting and they want to play, he'll grace them with his presence.

Q4. **You've got to dash into work unexpectedly and it means leaving the house when you'd normally be there. How does your pooch react?**

A She's sad you're leaving, but she's soon up to puppy mischief.

B She likes to have some doggy me-time.

C She thinks it's a good time to impress the neighbours with her vocal prowess.

D She allows you time off for good behaviour.

Q5. **How would you describe your dog's day-to-day demeanour?**

A This chirpy, chipper chappie is full of fun and love.

B Mr Cool and Calm, right down to the tip of his tail.

C From over excited to anxious – chaotic is the word.

D A woof above aloof, this pup is full of attitude!

Q6. **It's the day every dog dreads – the annual check-up at the vets – but how does yours deal with it?**

A She's not a fan, but as long as you're by her side she'll be ok.

B She takes it in her stride and enjoys the change of scenery.

C She has a full-on mutt meltdown.

D She's irritated and doesn't like to be handled by another human.

Q7. **On a day-to-day basis, what freaks out your dog the most?**

A A high-pitched siren makes his ears prick up.

B Nothing, he's a laidback lovely and confident in his own fur.

C Losing sight of you makes him yappy and snappy.

D He's not one for crowds of people.

Q8. **While you love every second you spend with your pooch, what's your favourite time of day to spend together?**

A We both get excited about walkies. The great outdoors and time together, what's not to love?

B Afternoon cuddles on the sofa are your happy place.

C At night, when she curls up and sleeps like a baby, sometimes using you for a pillow.

D Playtime is the A time. You get to see her relax and you join in the fun.

Q9. **It's holiday season and you're planning some time away. What do you do with your pup?**

A You take him with you. He loves to explore and he'll have lots of fun.

B You take him to the kennels. He's happy to go on his own staycation away from home.

C Holiday? What holiday? You won't leave this nervous lad with anyone.

D You leave him at home and pay for a dog sitter. That way he stays in charge and in his own space.

It's a Dog's Life

The Results

The Optimist
WELL-BALANCED & ADAPTABLE

This cheerful Charlie always has a spring in her step. She just loves every minute of his day, and while she responds best to routine, she's not averse to the odd curve ball if it means a new experience. Life is for living, and this mutt likes to fully engage. From sniffing roses to the rubbish bin, she'll stick her nose in everything. As far as she's concerned, wherever the nose goes, adventure flows, but it can also lead her into trouble. That said, she's not a naughty pooch, and her pleasant demeanour makes her the ideal playmate for human pups too. She's most likely an easy-going breed like a Beagle, Retriever or Bassett Hound, but don't let that fool you – this bow wow can bounce, so regular exercise and playtime is a must. A big fan of walkies, she'll expect it on the dot every day, so chop-chop, get your coat on and get ready to play!

It's a Dog's Life

The Dude

WELL-BALANCED & EXTROVERT

This laidback lad likes to go it alone. That doesn't mean he's not up for fun or a run, but he's more than happy to make his own entertainment. This boy's fur is the perfect fit, and he knows it. Outside stimulus or reassurance might be important for other mutts, but the Dude takes everything in his puppy dog stride. From sussing out new situations to valuing me-time and knowing the power of a good snooze, this mutt likes to channel some zen. If you're looking for a meditation partner or pooch pal to sit with and shoot the breeze, then he's your boy. Most likely a mellow French Bulldog or even a beautiful Bichon Frise, whatever breed he rocks, he's definitely not a working dog. He'll happily sit, stand or stroll at your side, but don't expect him to run and hide, or go wagtastically wild. He'd sooner slump in a hump than let anything get him riled.

The Panicker

INTROVERT & ADAPTABLE

This little character has it all going on. A big imagination and an anxious nature give this nervous nipper her signature style: crazy! She'll need a lot of gentle coaxing to bring her out of her shell and she'll quickly latch on to her owner, forming a lifelong bond. She'll dote on your every word and in return you'll have a partner in crime, because she'll rarely leave your side. That said, it's good to introduce a bit of space with some clever training techniques. Once she gets used to your occasional absence, she'll build confidence and be able to deal with other changes to the routine. Regular and often works well with this pooch, and play is important too, as it helps her work off some steam. Not one for strangers or playdates, this Freak-out Frida's only got eyes for one lucky person: you. She may be frenetic but she's a bundle of love wrapped in fur. Who could ask for more?

The Sulker

ADAPTABLE & INDEPENDENT

You never quite know where you stand with this moody mutt. One minute he's running like the wind, the next he's a huffy ball of fluff. It's not that he likes to keep you on your toes, it's just that he's a sensitive soul, even if he looks tough on the outside. His exterior is most likely impressive, and his face expressive. He's pretty vocal, as he'll try to express everything he thinks and feels, so listen up. Protective when it comes to you and the things he values, he doesn't like strangers or fuss, and knows instinctively when it's time for the vets. Breeds that fit this remit include Huskies, Jack Russells and Akitas, but their fierce attitude is all for show. Deep down this doggy delight just wants to do his own thing and enjoy family time, and anything that stops him getting his way is sure to ruin his day.

Pose Like a Pooch

What's Your Dog's Signature Style?

It's no surprise that humans have been breeding dogs for thousands of years. They're more than just man's best friend; our canny canines have skills and talents that we can't match, so our ancestors capitalized on this and bred them for size and speed. For some breeds, for example the Rottweiler, it's all about stature and dominance. Some dogs were created specifically to guard, making them protective and nurturing in nature, like the Mastiff or the capable German Shepherd. Others, like the sleek and speedy Greyhound, became exceptional hunting partners, and their inquisitive streak reflects this. Over time, the breeding process was refined, with tweaks that would eventually produce around 200 distinctive variations. No wonder our dogs come in all shapes and sizes!

Whether you're after a handsome hunter, a poser pooch or a manly mutt, you're sure to find your doggy match, but it pays to note the differences. From body shape to beauty needs, some pups love attention and care, while others prefer to go with what nature gave them. Whatever style your canine rocks, when you dig a little deeper you'll discover that what's on the surface can reveal so much more about what's underneath.

Q1. If you could sum up your pooch in a few words, how would you describe her?

A   Big, bold and beautiful.

B   A coy cutie.

C   A scallywag, wild and free.

D   Graceful and self-assured, like a prima ballerina.

Q2. From full-on pooch parties to a gambol in the countryside, there are many ways to celebrate your canine's birthday. Which would he prefer?

A   A run-around with his pooch pals on a field.

B   A game of dress-up, followed by a photo shoot.

C   A muck around in the mud on a long walk.

D   Pampering, cuddles and canine-friendly cake.

Pose Like a Pooch

Q3. What's your pooch's grooming routine like?

A As and when you can give her a quick scrub.

B She's the Pooch Parlour's top patron.

C Soil exfoliation and a pond dip bring out her feral charm.

D A regular shampoo and a brush every week and she's good to go.

Q4. They say that most owners look like their dog, but what would you have to do to accessorize with your dog?

A Throw on any old coat so you can head outside for some fun!

B We're in matching couture all the way.

C I already do when I tumble out of bed with messy hair.

D He's way too classy for human accessories.

Q5. A posh Pekingese might turn her nose up at muck, while a fun-loving Staffy might roll in it. Is your canine squeaky clean or a messy pup?

A She makes her mark wherever she ventures.

B She's a pampered, pretty princess.

C Mess is her middle name, along with muck, dirt and scruff.

D It's simple: clean and classy for this girl.

Q6. Style and swagger are second nature to some dogs, but how does your pup like to strut his stuff?

A He bounds, like a mutt with attitude.

B Whether in handbag or on lap, this cute pup likes to be carried in comfort.

C Rough and tumble is only way this pooch rolls.

D He glides on air, literally!

Q7. You're sharing a cosy cuddle with your canine. Is it a sweet-smelling dream or a whiffy nightmare?

A She's *all* dog, but you don't mind.

B Primped and preened, she's a perfumier's dream.

C Wild and wonderful, she smells of the earth.

D This odourless beauty is as fresh as a daisy.

Q8. If your pooch had a hashtag, it would be ...

A #WagtasticWonder

B #DoggyDiva

C #WolfAtHeart

D #BowWowBeauty

Pose Like a Pooch

63

Q9. How does your pup react to getting caught in a downpour?

A   A little rain doesn't hurt, but she's not a fan of a shower.

B   She has a meltdown. Who wants to be smelly and wet?

C   She loves, loves, loves it!

D   She tolerates it with style.

The
Results

A

The Showman

WELL-BALANCED & EXTROVERT

This gorgeous mutt knows how to make a mark, without even trying. Think bow wow, that wow wows! He doesn't have to work it, it's already there in the puppy dog stare and the whoosh of a tail that won't stop wagging. His enthusiasm is contagious; it has you and everyone else under his spell. Not that he wants to be in control; he's quite happy doing doggy stuff, and if you want to come along for the ride, that's fine by him. The way he looks is not as important as the way he feels. Most likely a sporting or hunting breed, or a smaller dog with big ideas, the Showman doesn't respond to platitudes. Instead, go bold and brave, and join in with the fun. Don't try and preen or even keep him clean; just get ready to run and run. He'll love having you at his side, and you'll soon realize that exercise and lots of fuss is what truly makes him shine!

Pose Like a Pooch

The Poser

EXTROVERT & ADAPTABLE

This girl's a Princess with a capital P. She knows it's all about the pooch, and rightly so! Whether she's sitting pretty on her velvet embossed recliner or nestled neatly in your designer bag, she likes to do everything in style. Life's too short to be anything but beautiful and she appreciates the time and care you take on her appearance. Other dogs have their strengths and talents, but this lady knows it's all about the pose. Most likely a toy breed, she's teeny tiny and at times a little whiny. Get her out of the handbag and on to the ground by playing games that intrigue her. Hide a treat in a toy and watch her inner huntress reveal itself. For a little dog, she has big standards and an even bigger attitude, so why settle for second best? That goes for you, too. As far as she's concerned, you're the top of the tree when it comes to human company.

C The Wild Child

DOMINANT & WELL-BALANCED

Wild and wonderful, that's how this boy runs. A free spirit, with a love for the great outdoors, the Wild Child understands the lure of the open road and could probably survive off-grid using his wits and ragamuffin charm. Beauty is just a word to him, and you'll soon realize that scruffy has its charms too. After all, there's something attractive about not giving a sausage when it comes to your appearance! If you're up for a challenge, then he'll certainly oblige, but don't expect it to be a walk in the park. When you run with this boy, you run with the wolves. Get him used to training slowly, and limit distractions by putting away toys and anything that might catch his eye. At the end of the day, you may be able to tame him, but don't expect the same of his fur. It's rough and tangled all the way!

Pose Like a Pooch

The Class Act

WELL-BALANCED & INDEPENDENT

Posed and polished, this lady has all the grace of a prima ballerina. Like a supermodel, she'll float into a room and become the centre of attention within seconds. No wild woofing for this wonder; her body language and uncompromising stare reveal her steel. At first glance, you might think she's somewhat coy, but don't let that fool you. She might not be flapping and yapping with the best of them, but she's still a force to be reckoned with. Hers is a quiet strength, tenacious and gracious, and able to hold her own. The Class Act responds well to training. She likes routine and regular exercise sessions, which help her stay toned and trim and also engage her sharp brain. Likely to be slender and muscular in frame, think Italian Greyhound or even a Saluki. Keep her clean and lean and she'll dance to your tune every day.

Pose Like a Pooch

Canine Smarts and Training

How Does Your Dog Respond To Instruction?

Training is one of the best ways to bond with your dog. It's one-on-one time when you can really get to know each other and learn how each other communicates. You'll also discover who's in charge – or who thinks they are! Training gives your pooch a challenge that engages them on many levels. They'll learn how to respond in different situations and they'll also get used to the tone of your voice.

Doggy intelligence varies from breed to breed, and some dogs take to training better than others. Working dogs who have a purpose will blossom; Border Collies especially enjoy the challenge. Hounds, on the other hand, tend to follow their nose rather than responding to orders. Their inquisitive nature means they're bright but more interested in sniffing out their own fun. Dogs like this need to know all the extra effort is worth it, so a pocket full of treats is a must. Then there are the doggy don'ts and won'ts: the ones who can, but aren't a fan of being told what to do, and the ones who need a little extra motivation.

Training can put a spring in your Spaniel's step, and will ensure your relationship is a well-balanced one. Looking at the way your dog responds to instruction will help you to learn how to get the best from them by working to their strengths.

Q1. **It's time to be honest. How much does your pooch enjoy training sessions?**

    A   You two are so in tune, it's a bonding exercise.

    B   You have to catch him first. This dude likes it his way or the highway.

    C   This over-excitable pooch laps up the fun even if it doesn't always go to plan.

    D   In a word, no. This pup is not for training!

Q2. **You're demonstrating your skills as a dog whisperer. You say 'sit' and your dog ...**

    A   Drops into a perfect squat.

    B   Jumps up your leg and nearly knocks you over.

    C   Manages to sit after the third attempt, with you directing her derriere.

    D   Looks at you like you've asked her to climb Mount Everest.

Q3. Is your pooch a master at tricks and turns, or is flopping on his belly the only act he likes to pull?

A He loves dancing and prancing at the click of your fingers.

B He's a master at slipping the lead.

C He can roll over if you tickle his tum.

D He's perfected the 'I am not amused' look.

Q4. You're taking a leisurely stroll with your pup, when she starts to growl at someone. What happens next?

A You tell her to stop, and she obeys, naturally!

B She snarls and you have to physically restrain her.

C You give her a stroke and she calms down.

D She stops growling and goes off in a sulk.

Q5. Your pooch wants a game of hunt the slipper, but you'd rather wear them. Who wins?

A It's a team effort, but really you wear the slippers and you put your foot down.

B You might as well buy a new pair; you'll never see that one again!

C There are no winners or losers in this game, it's back and forth until one of us gives up!

D He does – he eats it.

Q6. **You've decided to up your personal fitness and do a spot of circuit training in the garden. What does your dog do?**

A She joins in. A wagtastic workout with her human! What's not to love?

B She's more interested in digging up the garden.

C She's racing along the sidelines, barking encouragement.

D As far as she's concerned, it's doggy nap time.

Q7. **When you call your dog's name, he ...**

A Is already by your side, no summons required.

B Legs it in the opposite direction.

C Goes bananas, jumping up and down at the sound of your voice.

D Gives you that 'Yeah, so?' look.

Q8. **You're out walking your pooch on the lead. You want to go one way; your dog has other ideas. Who wins?**

A You. With a little gentle encouragement she'll go wherever you go.

B This pooch is already pounding the mean streets in the opposite direction!

C It's a spirited discussion involving lots of yaps, barks and tail wagging, but you win.

D Bottom to ground for the foreseeable – this girl won't budge unless you carry her!

Q9. **Training is a balance of encouragement, repetition and reward, but what works for one dog doesn't always work for another. What type of training does your pooch like the best?**

A Any. This dog loves to learn, and as long as there's action, he's ready!

B The little and often approach is the only way to go, as he's not a fan of training time.

C It's all about the treats with this pooch; tasty nibbles spur him on.

D This pup's only up for training when it's you that's jumping to his tune!

The Results

The Olympian
DOMINANT & WELL-BALANCED

This athletic girl is as bright as a button and fleet of foot. Throw in a wet nose and an ever-present wagging tail and you've got the full package. She won't let you down because she enjoys the challenge just as much as you do. Her brain needs stimulus and her limbs need to run; it's a simple equation but one that will keep this bow wow wowing. Not one to let the grass grow under her paws, she's off before you've even blown the starting whistle. Find a way to have fun together, from playing fetch games on an incline which make her work for the reward to seeking out new and interesting routes for walkies. You'll know when she's had enough when she comes in for a stroke. Most likely a working or hunting dog, she's able to think on the hoof, and is always a gold medal winner in your eyes.

The Rebel

EXTROVERT & INDEPENDENT

Training? What's that? It's not that this lad is lazy – far from it! He's razor sharp and raring to go, but in the opposite direction. Forget obedience, the only way that's going to work is if you do what he wants. You might think he's naturally naughty, but it's his freedom-loving streak that gets him into hot water. This canny canine lives by his wits, and it serves him well, but some training techniques to tame his erratic side would help both of you feel better. Try calm but firm commands, followed by lots of fuss and his favourite treat. Like any mutt, the Rebel loves attention almost as much as he loves getting one up on you, so educate with kindness and you'll see his gentler side shine through. It may be one step forward, two steps back, but slow and steady wins the training race and you'll both come out on top.

Canine Smarts and Training

79

The Jester
WELL-BALANCED & ADAPTABLE

She might not be top of the class, but what this girl lacks in sporty prowess, she more than makes up for in puppy finesse. Cute, cuddly and lots of fun, you may be pulling your hair out by the end of a session but you'll have had your share of giggles too. She tries her best but quickly loses interest when put to the test over and again. That said, it's worth persevering with this pooch, as once she masters something, it will stay with her forever. The Jester likes to keep you happy, and that's her main motivation in life, but should something more interesting and sniff-worthy take her fancy, then watch out world! Next door's barbeque or the cat from up the street will always take precedence to waiting at heel.

The Mutineer

DOMINANT & INDEPENDENT

If you're looking for the mutt who's most likely to jump ship at the thought of some exercise, look no further. There'll be no playing ball for this pup. He's a sit on the sidelines and snarl boy. That's not to say he's aggressive but getting hot under the collar is as appealing to him as having his nails trimmed. With his expressive features, he'll let you know he's not amused, and if that doesn't work, be prepared for the big sulk – a sit-in, backside to floor fashion, and done with passion. He may even run off elsewhere. If you want to tame his Mutineer ways, you've got your work cut out. From pulling a strop to turning up the cute factor, he'll try it all. Match his mind games with activities that make him think. Doggy puzzles will have him hooked, or a simple game of hide-and-seek should get him off his feet!

Woof and Tumble

How Does Your Dog Like To Play?

All dogs need exercise and time to play, but breed is a big influence on how much and the type of activity required. The Vizsla is a muscular powerhouse who loves long hikes, while a dog with shorter legs might struggle with rough terrain. If you're looking for speed, then Greyhounds with their long and graceful limbs are the ones to watch. They are able to reach up to 45mph, but as long as they get in a daily sprint, they'll be happy.

Your pup's approach to play also has an impact on their health and wellbeing, as this is a way to build exercise into their routine. Whether you have an independent pooch who likes to take the initiative or a lazy lass who prefers the party to come to her, every dog has their way of doing things. A cheeky and impatient dog might steal something of yours to start the chase, while an introverted and timid pup might take a back seat or even hide from sight. What makes your pup special is more than just how much they move, but this does reveal another facet of their personality – what they enjoy doing and how they feel when they're doing it. If you want an insight into the inner workings of your mutt's mind, look at their play style and what puts the wiggle in their walk.

Q1. When faced with a field and no lead, what does your pup do?

   A   She thinks she's in a race to reach the other side and goes full throttle.

   B   She likes to explore, jump and run for a bit, but soon runs out of steam.

   C   She looks for something to hunt!

   D   She'll amble along with you by her side.

Q2. What's your mutt's game of choice?

   A   Fetch, whether with a frisbee or tennis ball.

   B   Swipe the sausage off the barbeque.

   C   Chase the squirrel.

   D   Steal and hide the slipper.

Q3. After your usual walkies, you've decided to take a new, longer route home which involves lots of hills and rough terrain. How does your pooch cope?

   A   She's in her element, navigating it like an assault course.

   B   She's enthusiastic at the start, but soon gets fed up.

   C   She's distracted by all the new sounds and scents.

   D   She's not impressed and keeps stopping for a rest.

Q4. How resourceful is your dog when it comes to creating fun?

   A   Anything is fair game, from the washing line to the TV remote.

   B   If there's a discarded toy, he'll find a use for it.

   C   Insects beware; if it moves, he'll catch it!

   D   He prefers the fun to come to him.

Q5. When it comes to running with the pack, how does your pup fare?

   A   She's the leader of the pack and always out in front.

   B   She can keep up but prefers to dawdle at the back of the group.

   C   She enjoys chasing the other pups.

   D   She doesn't do running and prefers to watch from a safe distance.

Q6. **When presented with a new chewy bone toy, how does your pooch react?**

A Joy, joy, joy ... he'll play with it all day.

B He tries to eat it, naturally!

C If it doesn't move, he's not interested.

D He backs away from the alien object.

Q7. **Will your pup let strangers get in on the act when it comes to playtime?**

A Playtime is when she runs free, and she doesn't need anyone for that!

B Yes, if more people means more foodie treats.

C As long as they're up for a game of tag.

D No way, she's a one-human mutt.

Q8. **Your pooch is enjoying a nap in the afternoon sun when a butterfly lands on his nose. What's the likely outcome?**

A A game of hide-and-seek, with lots of spinning around.

B Takeaway snack, anyone?

C A frantic chase as dog tries to catch butterfly.

D He'll hide from the strange, winged assassin.

Woof and Tumble

Q9. You've accidently left out a pack of biscuit treats in the kitchen. What does your dog do?

A Takes a running leap and snaffles the pack.

B Jumps up and down until she eventually knocks them to the floor.

C Nothing. It's no fun when the snack isn't moving!

D She sits and whines until you realize your mistake and give her a treat.

The Results

The Sprinter

DOMINANT & WELL-BALANCED

On your marks, get set, run! That's the Sprinter's mantra, not that he needs much encouragement. Once his motor's running, there's no looking back. Sleek, chic and spirited, he's an athlete with a gold medal in mind. Long distances don't faze him; in fact, he relishes the challenge. Most likely a sporting breed such as a Setter or a Spaniel, his need to run is part of his make up, so be prepared for lots of exercise. If you're a runner yourself, he makes an excellent coach, spurring you onwards when the going gets tough. While he's not an armchair lounger, rest is important, as is play. Give him downtime by rewarding him when he's calm and resting with his favourite treats, so that he knows quiet time is good. For a fully rounded pup, he needs lots of attention, but in return he'll lead by example, and bring out your pooch potential!

Woof and Tumble

The Pleaser

WELL-BALANCED & ADAPTABLE

This joyful girl may not be the sportiest pooch in the pack, but she'll have a go with the right encouragement. Food is her main motivation, so throw in some of her favourite treats and it's game on. She's not likely to be the winner, but as long as she's first place in your heart, she's a happy lady. A desire to please and the promise of a juicy bone gets her up and moving. Other types of motivation work too, and tasty biscuit treats are not to be sniffed at. Shift the focus by playing games for two – she and you – and stick to low calorie nibbles to keep her waistline in check. She'll never leave you standing at the starting line, but she might leave you laughing at her playful antics. As far as breeds are concerned, she crosses barriers, from working to herding and toy; the Pleaser can be found in all of them.

The Hunter

EXTROVERT & INDEPENDENT

Prey is what plays upon this pup's mind. He's alert and ready to assert his will upon you. He loves to hunt, by spotting the object of his attention and racing off at speed. That's not to say he's aggressive; the Hunter loves the thrill of the chase, but it isn't a race. He will take his time and deviate from the plan should something more interesting come along. His finely tuned senses act like a radar, and this, coupled with his agility and often a short burst of speed, means he's always on target. His drive to succeed and snaffle the catch is the thing that powers him on. While he's likely to be a hunting breed like an Afghan Hound, many cross-breeds and smaller dogs, even Dachshunds, have this instinct too. Keep him sweet by changing things up and introducing new environments and toys to your play sessions.

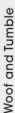

The Observer

INTROVERT & ADAPTABLE

This cautious girl likes to keep her distance. While other pups love the fun and bluster of a good run around, this pooch prefers the peaceful approach. She'll stand at the finish line and cheer on the pack; just don't expect her to join in. That's above her pay grade and, anyway, she's not made for sporty stuff. The world scares her at times, and until she gets to know the ins and outs of a thing, the jury's out and she's off. Encourage her to join in with gentle coaxing and reward any effort to play with a treat. Once she's familiar with something or someone, you'll see a different side to her. No more run and hide mutt, she'll sniff and stay put. She might even step up a gear and show some interest, but she's not one for jumping around. Life is to be enjoyed at a leisurely pace, not treated like a four-legged race.

Woof and Tumble

Pooch Power

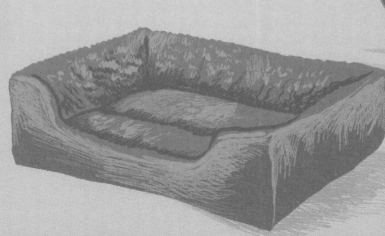

How Does Your Dog Relate To You?

Dogs are the empaths of the animal kingdom. They can easily pick up on our emotions and sense when we're ill. Our clever canines collate this information through body language, facial recognition and engaging their super honed sense of smell. Your pooch's sensitive snout sniffs out subtle shifts in scent, caused by hormones and disease, so they can tell when you're feeling low or in pain. While this goes a long way to explain the special bond you have with your fur buddy, there's even more going on in their doggy brain!

A dog's natural instinct is to please and to connect with their human. This, coupled with other urges which surface in specific breeds – like the need to protect, nurture or guard often seen in Dobermans and German Shepherds – means they'll go the extra mile to understand and engage with you. Dogs like to mirror their owners, and they can sniff out danger and instinctively know when you need a helping paw. No wonder they're man's best friend. The strong connection between you makes them feel comfortable, so they're more likely to reveal their true pawsonality and what's really going on behind their puppy dog eyes. By looking at the way they relate to you, you'll learn more about your pup's nature and how to repay their generosity in kind.

Q1. You're feeling under the weather. How does your dog react?

A   Your pain is his pain, and he quietly consoles you.

B   He rallies you with fuss and frolics.

C   He's curled up there alongside you.

D   He's wary and keeps his distance.

Q2. You're finally home from a long day at work. What's the first thing your pup does when you walk through the door?

A   She's already at the window, watching and waiting for your return.

B   She's circling her food bowl, to remind you it's teatime.

C   She jumps on you at the door and nearly knocks you over.

D   She barks and wags her tail as if to say, 'At last, you're back!'

Q3. Dogs communicate in many different ways, but how do you know when your dog is saying 'I love you'?

A   He gives you the long lingering look of love.

B   He jumps up and nuzzles you.

C   He goes in for a zealous face lick.

D   He rubs and leans against you so that you can feel his presence.

Q4. They say owners often resemble their pooch, but just how similar are the two of you?

A   We're two peas in the pod. We totally 'get' each other.

B   We might not always act the same, but we do understand one another.

C   I'm in charge and she follows my lead.

D   We complement and look out for each other.

Q5. There's someone banging at the door, and it makes you jump. How does your dog react?

A   He calmly stays by your side.

B   He leaps in the air, then the yapping begins.

C   He whines and whimpers.

D   He puts on his best guard dog snarl and barks aggressively.

Q6. **You've had a stressful day, and you're still feeling pretty wound up. What does your dog do?**

A She perches next to you on the sofa so that you can stroke her.

B She brings you her lead. A walk will do you both good!

C She presents her tum for a restorative tickle.

D She curls up close by and keeps a watchful eye.

Q7. **You're catching up with a group of friends in the park. How does your dog react when you wander off?**

A It's no big deal, he just trots behind you.

B He takes the opportunity to have a wander himself.

C He turns into the woof monster and makes a racket.

D He's at your heel, checking in before you know it.

Q8. **A stranger crashes into you on the street, knocking you sideways. What does your pooch do?**

A She sticks to your leg and emits a low growl.

B She barks at the top of her voice.

C She gets panicky and starts whimpering.

D She stands in front of you and bares her teeth.

Q9. **You've had some fantastic news and you're super excited. How does your pup react?**

A He senses your joy and matches it with lots of tail wagging.

B He makes the most of your mood and brings you his favourite toy.

C He picks up on the vibe, but it makes him nervy.

D He gives you his best 'calm down' bark.

The
Results

2
5

The Bestie

WELL-BALANCED & ADAPTABLE

Sensitive and sweet, the Bestie seems to know what you're thinking before you do. You are the apple of her eye, and as such, she makes it her mission to know everything about you. Attuned to your scent, her powers of observation are second to none, and wherever you go, she'll be there reading the room and making sure you're alright, without being overprotective or clinging to your side. Words are not needed here! Body language says it all and you mirror each other perfectly. Whether you're in need of space, a furry shoulder to cry on or just a right-hand pup to back you up when the going gets tough, the Bestie is sure to respond in kind. Relationships like this tend to come once in a lifetime, so treasure this bond and make lots of wonderful memories together.

Pooch Power

2 3

B

The Furry Godmother

WELL-BALANCED & EXTROVERT

If you're feeling low, this dog's sure to gee you up. He seems to know what's best for you and has a knack of delivering this wisdom in ways that make you smile. Feeling sluggish? He'll be the one 'nosing' you out the door for a brisk walk. After all, the Furry Godmother 'knows' that what is good for you is good for him too. He can sniff out the changes in your body and has enough bounce for the both of you. If you're looking for a cheerleader, this boy fits the bill. He'll be on the sidelines barking encouragement and whooping it up when you succeed. He likes to make some noise, but his enthusiasm is contagious and sometimes it's just what you need to lift the spirits. While he might not always understand you, the Furry Godmother has your best interests at heart; it's his mission to put the woof in your walk.

Pooch Power

103

The Cherub

INTROVERT & ADAPTABLE

This cutie makes your heart melt. She looks to you for guidance in all things. If you're alright, she's alright, but should you flounder, this pup turns to mush. Like most dogs, she's an empath and knows exactly what you're feeling. She can sense danger, but instead of going all out to protect, this only alarms her. She feels your pain and makes it her own until she's in a tizz of a tailspin. The Cherub needs reassurance and may suffer separation anxiety, even when you step out of the room. Training and encouragement are the key to her confidence. Create a special space with her bed and favourite things and encourage her to spend some time there without you every day. She'll never be assertive, but she will learn that things aren't so bad when you're not immediately by her side. That said, this pup knows how to give a sloppy cuddle, and there's nothing you like more than a bow wow love-in.

The Bodyguard

DOMINANT & INDEPENDENT

This boy takes his role in life very seriously. He's made it his mission to protect you at all costs, and in return you'll be his companion and best human. It's a match made in heaven as far as he's concerned. Gifted with keen observation skills and the ability to sense subtle shifts in atmosphere, this lad never lets his guard slip. Loyal and loving, the Bodyguard won't back down from a challenge and will do everything in his power to keep you safe. While he's not as soppy as some, it doesn't mean he doesn't care. He shows it in other ways. His steady, reassuring presence is all you need to feel instantly brighter and lighter. Athletic in build, he's likely to have been bred as a guard dog, but he's also your pooch pal, and with lots of love and bonding activities he'll soon realize that looking out for each other is a two-way street.

Pooch Power

Dogs on the Move

How Great Is Your Dog's Sense Of Adventure?

Dogs are doers. They love to be on the go, sniffing out mischief and using their super honed senses to engage with the world around them. With a nose that uses each nostril separately to smell in 3D, and a hearing range that far excels that of a human, it's no wonder mutts seek stimulus in the form of new adventure! Whether they're just having a run around in your garden or hitting the local park with a passion, most pooches love the great outdoors, although there are always exceptions. Some dogs have a fear of what's out there, depending on their experience of the wider world. If they're a rescue dog, then it's no surprise that once they find their forever home, they don't want to leave it, but even these types of pups can be encouraged to enjoy what lies on the other side of the door, as long as you're by their side.

Confidence is key when it comes to exploring. The cautious pup seeks reassurance, while the inquisitive soul is off the minute you've slipped the lead. And let's not forget the car – some dogs love a road trip! Wherever your dog fits on the adventure scale, what they do once they're on the move reveals how spontaneous and outgoing they can be, and also how comfortable they are in an environment that's constantly changing.

Q1. **You've been out on a walk and home is in sight. What does your dog do?**

A She looks around for something to sniff or chase; anything to prolong her adventure outside.

B She barks with joy and rubs up to your leg.

C She tries to break free by pulling on her lead in the opposite direction.

D She goes full pelt and drags you up to the front door.

Q2. **How does your dog walk with you on the lead?**

A He's constantly wandering off in different directions.

B At heel, in perfect time with your own gait.

C He drags you along at a pace.

D Reluctantly. This pooch likes to plod.

Dogs on the Move

Q3. **As much as your mutt craves routine, it can be good to mix things up. What's your dog's favourite exercise route?**

A A higgledy-piggledy trek through the woods.

B A gentle stroll through the park that you can enjoy together.

C Open fields where she can run far and fast.

D Familiar streets that lead to home.

Q4. **You've turned your back for a moment. What's your dog likely to do?**

A Look around for interesting whiffs to sniff.

B Stay by your side, waiting for you to notice him.

C Make his escape. You won't see him for dust!

D Grab the opportunity for an on-the-spot scratch.

Q5. **You've taken your dog somewhere new for the first time. How does she react?**

A Her nose is twitching, her tail is wagging, she can't wait to explore.

B She's nervous at first, but with some gentle coaxing she starts to relax.

C She scopes the territory to get her bearings, then she's off.

D She shares her displeasure by whining loudly.

Q6. **What's your pup's favourite day out?**

A   A trip to the countryside.

B   A mosey around the shops with you.

C   He loves a day at the beach.

D   A date at your local café, with the promise of a foodie treat.

Q7. **Is your pooch a water baby, or a land lover?**

A   If there's something of interest in the water, then she'll dive in.

B   She's a fan of terra firma; water freaks her out.

C   All day every day, this pooch loves a good splash about.

D   She'll hide beneath the surface of the water when you're calling her.

Q8. **On your travels together, you get chatting to a stranger, but how does your mutt react?**

A   He's excited to make a new friend and goes in for a sniff and a lick.

B   His protective instinct kicks in and he barks loudly.

C   He's frustrated that this person is taking up valuable run time and tugs at his lead.

D   He slumps behind you in a grump.

Q9. You're venturing further afield and have decided to take your pooch in the car, but what kind of passenger is she?

A Her head is out of the window and her tail is wagging – this is one happy camper.

B Curled up foetal style, she'll stay in her cage and ride it out.

C Pacing and whining, she wants to be outside, rather than trapped in a metal carriage.

D As long as she doesn't have to do anything, she's fine watching the world whizz by.

The Results

The Thrill-Seeker

DOMINANT & EXTROVERT

Life is a roller coaster, and this lad loves to ride it! He knows that every minute of every day is packed with potential, from new smells and sounds to delicious bites and foraged finds that make his tail tingle. He likes to break new ground, and if that means breaking the rules, so be it. This mighty mutt woofs in the face of fear, and while he can take instruction, he prefers to go his own way. That said, if you take him to pastures new, he'll return the favour by keeping you entertained with his antics. His sense of smell, coupled with the need to explore, means he's likely to be a Pointer or Spaniel, but even if that's not his breed, he's raring to go. Friendly and inquisitive, you can keep him at his tail-wagging best by upping the training ante. Set him daily challenges and he'll thrive. This is one pup who's up for anything!

Dogs on the Move

The Ambler

WELL-BALANCED & ADAPTABLE

This girl isn't a huge fan of the great outdoors – she can take it or leave it, but that doesn't mean she lacks a sense of fun. At your side is where it's at, and as long as you're happy, she's happy too. The relationship you share is built on time and trust; being with you makes her feel safe. Always eager to please, she delights in the simple things, from a gentle stroll to the shops to a game of fetch in the park. She doesn't need to wander far because she has everything she needs, and while her curiosity may be piqued by outside smells, this pooch prefers to pootle at her own speed and on a lead, to be sure you're only a paw's width away. Security is at the forefront of her mind, and should you feel threatened in any way, she'll cast aside her own fears and unleash the inner beast, so that everyone knows you are hers, and hers alone!

Mostly
C

The Escapee

WELL-BALANCED & INDEPENDENT

Run, run and then some: that's this boy's motto in all things. Most likely an athletic breed like a Setter or Saluki, he's able, agile and just loves to stretch his limbs. The open road doesn't scare him, in fact the more space the better, because once in his stride there's no stopping him. If you're planning to take him out, get your running shoes on, and make sure you're in tip-top condition too. You won't be able to keep up, but at least you'll be able to keep him in your sights. Being within four square walls is not his happy place, and he'll need regular and lengthy bouts of exercise to satisfy his need for pace. Once the zip has gone from his zoom and he's all worn out, he'll take comfort in your company and some tasty treats.

Dogs on the Move

The Sloth

DOMINANT & WELL-BALANCED

You might think this girl is lazy, and you'd be right! The sofa is her best friend, along with her bed, your bed and any other soft surface that moulds to fit her form. When it comes to adventure, she missed the memo, but that's fine. She's more than happy with her lot, especially if that includes lots of fuss and cuddles with you. That said, she'll reluctantly go along for the ride, but don't expect her to be full of the joys of spring. This couch potato will make it known in whatever way possible that's she's not a happy girl, from her down in the mouth expression to her laboured trudge or, worse still, her refusal to budge. Secretly, she enjoys the fresh air, but she just prefers to stand or sit and take in the view, while you do all the hard work. This pooch knows that exercise equals effort, and she's too busy doing nothing to care.

The Canine Six Score Page

Although your dog may not fit perfectly into one category, you can try and identify their key traits from the six canine characteristics (see page 9). You may find it's easy to guess if your pooch scores highly in the same areas; alternatively, their characteristics could be scattered over all six categories. Either way, identifying the most dominant traits will give you an idea of your dog's true nature and what drives them, which will help you adopt the right approach when training and building a relationship together.

Below are the six characteristics featured in the profiles at the end of the quizzes. Leave a tick or a mark each time your dog matches a trait, and keep score to discover your dog's main personality type:

1. Dominant
....
Total: ....

2. Well-balanced
....
Total: ....

3. Extrovert
....
Total: ....

4. Introvert
....
Total: ....

5. Adaptable
....
Total: ....

6. Independent
....
Total: ....

Conclusion

The quizzes in this book are designed to help you better understand your dog, and to give you an insight into their character and quirks. It's important to get to know how your pooch thinks, feels and relates to you, as just as you wish to understand them at a deeper level, they too seek to form a special bond with you.

While personality tests can help you delve into your pup's psychological make up, there is so much more to take into consideration. Just like humans, dogs are constantly evolving and learning how to co-exist with us. Their daily behaviour is influenced by how they feel, both emotionally and physically, as well as external aspects such as past experiences and what is going on around them. Changes within their environment can have an effect on their personality, particularly if they prefer routine, and they'll also pick up on how you're feeling.

This book provides a starting point from which you can explore your mutt's true nature and discover ways in which to help them live their best life. If they need more stimulus, you can provide it with regular play sessions that include puzzles and hidden treats to engage their mind. If your pup suffers with separation anxiety, you can practise time spent apart by withdrawing to another room for a few minutes, building this up gradually day by day.

By getting to know a little more about what makes them tick, you'll know how to motivate them and lift their mood, and also how to make them feel safe, secure and loved. You'll also know when there's something wrong, or if they're up for fun, fun, fun. Of course, nothing is set in stone and dogs can be full of surprises, but that's what makes them a joy to live with and lifelong companions to treasure. Enjoy the adventure!

Discover More

Dog Types and Breeds

With around 400 different, recognizable types of dog in the world, there's a canine companion for everyone! Your choice of breed depends on what kind of pooch you'd like to share your life with and what you have to offer. Where you live and who you live with also has some bearing, as well as how much time and training you can provide.

If you know what type of dog you're looking for and what you can give in return, you'll be able to find the best choice for you. Dogs, like humans, come in all shapes and sizes. Some dogs look pretty, while others are witty and super smart. There are those who sniff out trouble from a great distance and those who excel as part of a team, driven by power and purpose.

To help you find the right one, dog breeds are split into categories which describe why they were bred, and this will give you an insight into their natural instincts and impulses. Check out the list on the following pages, which includes some of the more familiar breeds, and see how your dog matches up to its profile and type.

Canine Categories

Designer dogs

These are not generally recognized as breeds in their own rights, as they are cross-breeds which combine the attributes of existing breeds. Hence, they are not bred for any particular purpose. Their loving and gentle personalities make them very popular, and their names generally reveal their ancestry, such as the Puggle (Pug x Beagle). Expect signs of both parents to emerge in these puppies, although their appearance can be very variable. Poodles play a part in the ancestry of many such crosses.

Breeds include: Labradoodle, Puggle, Cockapoo, Yorkiepoo

Suggested profiles: The Class Act, The Ambler

Gun dogs

These loving dogs are extremely sociable and friendly. Originally bred as hunting companions, they are multi-skilled, being able to hunt, locate and retrieve game for their owners.

Breeds include: English Setter, Pointer, Cocker Spaniel, Golden Retriever

Suggested profiles: The Optimist, The Hunter

Hounds

Originally bred to assist in hunting, these dogs fall into one of two categories: sight or scent hounds. They use their exceptional eyesight or highly honed sense of smell to catch prey.

Breeds include: Afghan Hound, Basset Hound, Beagle, Irish Wolfhound

Suggested profiles: The Thrill-Seeker, The Rebel

Pastoral

Nurturing and highly active, pastoral dogs were bred with herding and protection in mind. They are used all over the world to look after livestock such as sheep, cattle and reindeer, and to keep them safe from other predators.

Breeds include: Border Collie, German Shepherd, Finnish Lapphund, Old English Sheepdog

Suggested profiles: The Olympian, The Bodyguard

Terrier

Feisty and action-orientated, Terriers were originally bred to hunt and kill vermin. Their predatory nature means they have tremendous energy and need a lot of stimulation to feel happy. They may also not always see eye-to-eye with other dogs, particularly fellow Terriers.

Breeds include: Bull Terrier, Jack Russell Terrier, Fox Terrier, Staffordshire Bull Terrier

Suggested profiles: The Workaholic, The Wild Child

Toy

These small (sometimes tiny!) dogs were bred specifically as companions, originally to wealthy people and royalty. Unlike most other types, they're not bred with a job in mind, but their sweet nature makes them easy to bond with.

Breeds include: Bichon Frise, Cavalier King Charles Spaniel, Pomeranian, Pug

Suggested profiles: The Poser, The Bestie

Working

These dogs are bred with a specific job in mind, which could be anything from guarding or sled-pulling to rescuing people in danger. They're strong, hardworking and focused, but they can also be gentle giants.

Breeds include: Boxer, German Pinscher, Newfoundland, St Bernard

Suggested profiles: The Pleaser, The Guru

Further Reading

David Alderton, *The Right Dog for You*, Ivy Press (2021)

Lili Chin, *Doggy Language: A Dog Lover's Guide to Understanding your Best Friend*, Hachette (2020)

Sina Eschenweber, *Mental Exercise for Dogs: 101 Best Dog Games for Agility, Intelligence & Fun* (2020)

The Monks of New Skete, *How to Be Your Dog's Best Friend: The Classic Training Manual for Dog Owners*, Little, Brown (1998)

Kyra Sundance, *101 Dog Tricks: Step by Step Activities to Engage, Challenge, and Bond with your Dog*, Quarry Books (2007)

Daniel Tatarsky, *How Dogs Work: A Head-to-Tail Guide to your Canine*, DK (2021)

www.akc.org
Fantastic website covering all things canine, including types of dog and breed information.

www.bringfido.com
Wherever you're going, this website lists dog-friendly places, from hotels to top eateries.

www.dogstrust.org.uk
From giving a dog its forever home to finding out more about training and care, this website has it all.

www.rover.com/blog
A comprehensive website that provides handy tips and advice for life with dogs.

www.rspca.org.uk/advice andwelfare/pets/dogs
Practical advice on looking after your dog from top experts.

About The Author

Alison Davies writes for a wide selection of magazines and has penned over forty books on a variety of topics including animals, astrology and self-help. Her doggy credentials include the bestselling book *Be More Dog*, and she writes regularly on the subject of all things pooch for *Take a Break Pets*.

About The Illustrator

Alissa Levy of @LevysFriends is originally from Kyiv, Ukraine, but now lives and works in Germany. Her work centres around humans, their pets and their wonderful and ridiculous relationships.

Brimming with creative inspiration, how-to projects, and useful information to enrich your everyday life, quarto.com is a favourite destination for those pursuing their interests and passions.

First published in 2022 by White Lion Publishing,
an imprint of The Quarto Group.
The Old Brewery, 6 Blundell Street
London, N7 9BH,
United Kingdom
T (0)20 7700 6700
www.Quarto.com

A catalogue record for this book is available from the British Library.

ISBN   978 0 7112 6863 0
Ebook ISBN 978 0 7112 6865 4

10 9 8 7 6 5 4 3 2 1

Publisher   Jessica Axe
Commissioning Editor Zara Anvari
Senior Editor   Laura Bulbeck
Project Editor   Bella Skertchly
Designer   Josse Pickard

Printed in China

MIX
Paper from
responsible sources
FSC® C016973